Why Are You Looking at Me?

I Just Have Down Syndrome.

By Lisa Tompkins

Illustrated by Ryan Eubanks

D1297797

AuthorHouse™
1663 Liberty Drive
Bloomington, IN 47403
www.authorhouse.com
Phone: 1-800-839-8640

Published by AuthorHouse 01/26/2013

ISBN: 978-1-4817-1138-8 (sc)
*   978-1-4817-1139-5 (e)*

Library of Congress Control Number: 2013901684

Any people depicted in stock imagery provided by Thinkstock are models,
and such images are being used for illustrative purposes only.
Certain stock imagery © Thinkstock.

This book is printed on acid-free paper.

authorHOUSE®

Hi, my name is Lynn.

Do I look different to you? I might.

You see, I have something called Down Syndrome. It makes me look different than most people. It is not catchy like a cold or the flu.

I may be shorter than most people my age.

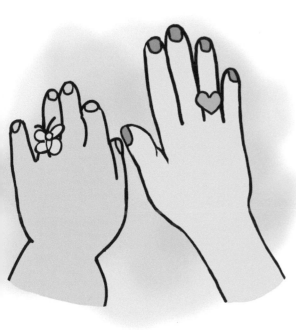

My feet and hands are smaller, too.

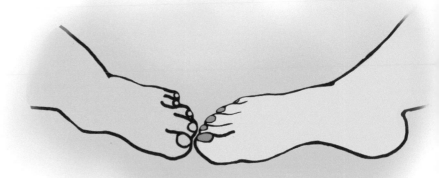

My eyes may be a different shape than yours.

But, that's okay because my smile and my laugh are the same.
I like to laugh.

I like to do what most kids my age do. I go to school,

swim . . .

Watch TV,

listen to music . . .

Go to church,

color . . .

Run . . .

Pretend,

dance . . .

Sing and even go to camp.

But my favorite thing to do is laugh and play
with my friends.

My friends, family and I have so much fun together, that
they don't even notice that I look a little different than
they do. Actually, it doesn't matter to them, because being
different, is being me!

Being me is fun. Sometimes I need help
reading and writing.

But, if anyone needs help in the kitchen, I am the right person for the job!

I am also pretty good at making my own bed and
folding my laundry.

I like to go shopping with my mom, too.

Whenever we go out, it is very hard for me. People who don't know me, or about my Down Syndrome, stare at me. I know they don't mean to hurt my feelings, but they do. Sometimes I want to ask them, "Why are you looking at me?".

If I asked you, what would you say?

Some people are missing out on all the fun of being my friend because they don't understand why they are looking at me.

I hope you understand me, so we can smile . . .

And laugh . . .

And be friends!

CPSIA information can be obtained
at www.ICGtesting.com
Printed in the USA
BVHW090225240721
612596BV00002B/19